The Judge

Landlord Coach Presents:

The Judge:
A Landlord's Tale

By Mark Dolfini

Dedication

To those who dare to act. To those having the courage to move toward your dreams. Don't lose sight of your Vision; keep your foot on the gas.

This is a story about a landlord. One you might know. One you might relate to.

Chapter One

Meet Bill. Bill owns rental property, which he manages himself. Although retirement is still quite a few years away, he started investing in real estate for when he quits working. Bill is fortunate to be in good health, so he's in no rush to leave his current job. However, if he could expand his real estate portfolio, he'd very much consider leaving work sooner than later. Bill has a little flexibility to take off when necessary, though he's never really had to take advantage of it. While at work, he handles phone calls and text messages from his residents here and there, but no one seems to notice.

In the beginning, Bill managed his first property quite well. He spent a few nights after work and a full weekend doing some light painting and cleaning and showing it to prospective tenants, and had the house rented within a week. Placing an ad in the paper and on Craigslist, he listed his personal cell phone for people to contact him. Bill scheduled property showings in half-hour increments, and people were scheduled to come scattered throughout the weekend: the first at

11:00 a.m., the next at 12:30 p.m., then at 4:00 p.m. and 4:30 p.m. Some wanted to see the house as late as 8:00 p.m. on Saturday and as early as 7:00 a.m. on Sunday. Bill didn't think to get anyone's contact information.

Most of the prospects showed up, but for those who didn't, Bill had no number to call to see if they were lost, running late, changed their mind, or just plain forgot. It didn't matter though, Bill was excited about his new business, admiring how easy this had all been so far. For those prospects who did show, he was able to meet them at the door and often spent over an hour getting to know them. Everyone was smiling and laughing and having a good time. Some prospects asked for a few things to be done to the house which seemed quite reasonable. "Sure thing," Bill answered, not thinking to write anything down, "I'll remember that stuff," he thought to himself. He also thought, on a few occasions, "What nice people, I hope I hear back from them..."

Some people asked Bill questions about the lease, but he wasn't really sure how to respond, as he didn't have one yet. He figured he'd download one from the internet or reference a copy of the lease he signed in college. Others asked about an application or an application fee, but he told them he didn't have one and to not worry about filling one out. He would just need to see a copy of their driver's license so he could fill out their names properly on the lease and check the public records for any evictions they may have had. He didn't have a way of pulling credit reports, so he told people not to worry about them. A few asked about the security deposit. He remembered hearing somewhere that one month's rent for the deposit was standard, so that's what he went with.

In spite of the few hiccups, it all went quite well. Actually, it was all pretty easy. So easy, in fact, Bill figured he could add to his portfolio without any disruption to his current lifestyle or impact on his life at work. He didn't mind spending a little time outside of his normal eight-to-five job performing maintenance here and there; he actually enjoyed doing that sort of work. It was a nice departure from the boredom he experienced sitting at his desk on the phone all day.

Several months went by, and Bill found a few more properties to purchase. By the end of three years, he had five properties for a total of six units: Four single family homes and one duplex. Things were going well. His cell phone rang more often than he was used to, but it was exciting for him to hear this affirmation of his real estate business growing so rapidly. Bill's friends got used to the interruptions at their weekly card game and started a running joke that he was actually a drug dealer. In spite of the burgeoning demand for Bill's attention, it was all very manageable, and he loved the attention he got from being called a "real estate mogul" by his close friends. Nothing called in by his tenants was horrible. Most issues he could handle very easily either over the phone or after work. Sometimes, his tenants called to invite him over for dinner or an occasional birthday party celebration. He prided himself on his relationships and how well he knew his tenants, their friends, even the names of their pets. It was a "people business" after all, and he enjoyed the service part of what he was doing.

One day at work, Bill is in a meeting with his boss and all the other department managers in attendance. Just about the time he is to stand and give his presentation, his cell phone rings. Fumbling through his jacket pocket, he sends the call to voicemail. Without looking up, Bill can feel the glaring eyes from the presenter standing at the head of the conference table, as well as from a few of his coworkers annoyed by the disruption. Before he can mute his phone, it rings again; this time he noticed it was his tenant. Sending it to voicemail once again, he barely gets the phone silenced before it's ringing again for a third time. Assuming the first two calls were from his tenant, he figured this must be an emergency. Excusing himself from the meeting, Bill steps outside as his phone persists.

"Hello," he half-whispers as he steps into the bustling hallway outside the conference room. "Bill, it's Margaret, we've got a big problem over here at the house…" Before he can process any more of his tenant's conversation, he's interrupted by a coworker, motioning for him to come back to the meeting. "Bill, we're all waiting for you."

Random words make their way through the phone "…our rent will be late…", "…not sure when we'll get paid…", "…wanted to let you know…", "…you've been so good to us…"

Finally, Bill gets control of the conversation, "Margaret, I'm really sorry to interrupt, but I'm at work and I really need to call you back." Closing out the conversation, he returns to the meeting where he tries his best to gather his thoughts and be present for the meeting. "Everything okay?" his boss chimes in from the head of the table. Unsure if he's going to have to raid his savings again to make the mortgage payment that month, Bill lies to his boss, "Sure, sorry for the interruption, just a call from a friend. Everything is okay."

Bill is fumbling with his papers as he takes his place at the front of the room – his turn to present his department's sales figures for that month. With everything in order, he proceeds, pointing to the screen where his slide presentation is being projected. "Okay everyone, sorry for the brief delay; let's get started..." his voice trailing off as he turns away from the screen to realize, suddenly, he was speaking to an empty room.

The chairs around the conference table had been pushed in and the table had been completely cleared. Not a sound could be heard from the usually kinetic office space outside the conference room. "Where did everyone go?" he thought to himself. The light whirring of the video projector fan being the only sound he could hear.

Walking across the room to the door, he listened carefully for the usual sounds of conversations and phones ringing. "Nothing," he thought. Turning the knob to the conference room door, he realized it was locked, or at least, it wouldn't turn. "This knob doesn't lock, what the heck is going on?" he thought out loud. This was the same door he just used to take the call from his tenant in the hallway.

"It's not going to open," he heard from a voice inside the room. Startled, Bill spun around and saw an older man sitting in the chair at the head of the conference table. The man was leaned back in the chair, his feet on the table and crossed at the ankles. A giant cigar in his mouth, he billowed blue-grey smoke into the air above his head.

"I'm sorry, who are you?" Bill stuttered, surprised at the sudden presence of his visitor. "And what's wrong with the door?"

"I'm The Judge," the man explained in a distinctly thick southern accent. "I wouldn't worry about that old door for the moment; you've got bigger fish to fry right now young man." His voice was deep and gristly, but he spoke fast. It was easy to tell that he meant business.

"The Judge?" Bill thought to himself, "Was this a new client?"

"No, I'm not a new client," the man replied to Bill's thoughts. "C'mon now Bill, you're an intelligent man, what kind of client comes to a meeting wearing a judge's robe around these parts?"

"Wait, you just read my mind. How did you…" Bill thought it was pointless to even finish his sentence. This whole situation was just bizarre. He attempted to gather his thoughts as he surveyed his guest's attire. Maybe he was dreaming. Bill thought it best to change the subject.

"You're from Texas?" Bill deduced from his southern accent.

"Alabama actually, but that's not important right now. What *is* important is the information I have to tell you and why I'm here". The man puffed at his cigar, only removing it to inspect the burning cherry and rotate it to ensure it's even burn.

"You can't smoke that in here," Bill protested flatly, "it's against company policy."

"Young man, who's smoking? Do you smell anything?"

In spite of the room filling with a haze of the man's cigar, Bill had to admit, there was no odor of cigar smoke.

"Exactly," the man settled, again reading Bill's thoughts. "Now, as I was saying, you've got something headed your way like thirty head-a-cattle chased by a swarm of hornets. So, unless you want to get stampeded, I'd strongly suggest you heed what I'm about to pass along."

"Um, okay…" Bill hesitated. "Are you a ghost or something? What do you need to pass along that's so urgent?"

"Son, I'm The Judge. I sat on the bench overseeing small claims, mostly evictions and landlord-tenant cases, for over 40 years. That is, until I was called to serve on a much Higher Bench".

"So, you went to the Supreme Court?" Bill queried.

"Well, something like that, but again, not really important right now," The Judge explained. Taking his feet off the table for the first time and leaning forward, he continued, "What you need to know is that you're going to be visited three times today. I recommend you mind your visitors carefully and pay them close attention. There are things you need to know while you still have time."

Before Bill could ask, the man chimed back in with his thick southern accent, "It don't matter who these three folks are, just that you will be visited and you will need to pay close attention. The direction and future of your life and many others depends on it."

"What in the world to you mean, '*While you still have time?*'" Bill knew he was working hard lately, but had he truly lost it?

Putting his hand to his face, Bill squinted tightly as he pinched both eyes with his thumb and forefinger. "Okay, I'll play along..." he said aloud.

Opening his eyes, Bill was standing in the front of the conference room once again; all of his coworkers and his boss had rejoined him. The Judge was gone, as was the descending haze of cigar smoke in the room. The bustle outside the room had resumed, along with the sound of the phones and office noise. His sales figures in his hand, the attendants of the room listening intently, waiting for him to deliver his presentation.

"Play along with what?" his boss asked, confused.

"I'm sorry," Bill confessed, realizing he was back in front of his coworkers ready to deliver his presentation. "I just have a terrible headache all of a sudden. I'll get through it; let's get started."

Bill delivered his summary, and the meeting quickly ended. Before leaving, one of his close work friends, Jessica, grabbed him by the sleeve and asked him if everything was okay. "Yeah sure, I just didn't sleep well last night I guess," Bill explained. "I'll be fine."

Jessica was a good friend to Bill. She looked out for him, and always worried about Bill's well-being and future with the company. This was especially true lately, as Bill seemed a lot more distracted at work since he started ramping up his real estate investments this past year. "Well, you've been getting a lot of personal calls on your cell phone lately. And today you seemed fine until you got that call earlier," Jessica explained. "You sure you're alright?"

"Yeah, Jessica; seriously it's nothing. I do appreciate your concern, but I'll be fine." Bill did appreciate Jessica's concern, but what business was it of hers that his cell phone rang during the day. "I get my work done," he thought to himself. "They just need to stay out of my personal business. They're just jealous that I have real estate, and eventually won't need this place."

"Well, it's just that there's talk around the office of how disruptive it is when you're constantly getting personal calls. I just want to know if there's something I can do to help," Jessica offered.

"No offense, Jessica, but everybody needs to stay out of my business. I get my work done. I mean, if they had a problem, why aren't they coming to me?" Bill was aggravated. Turning and walking away from his friend, he threw his hands in the air for effect.

Storming into the bathroom, Bill checked all the stalls to be sure he was alone. Turning to the sink, he splashed cold water onto his face, wondering if he was hallucinating and hoping he would snap out of it. "Alabama Judge", he said to himself, shaking his head, snorting and giving himself a smirk in the mirror.

After gaining his composure, he realized his phone was still on silent. Eight missed calls, all from his tenants. Several unread text messages were also in his phone. He didn't want to look, but he opened the application to see who they were from as he walked out into the hallway.

As he stepped out of the bathroom, he noticed something was immediately different. The collective busyness of the office had again been replaced. This time, instead of silence, it was the sound of a child laughing and playing in what seemed to be someone's living room. Bill looked around at the unfamiliar scene, turning to go back through the bathroom door from which he came, but it held firm.

"What is going ON with me!" he exclaimed, frustrated by his lack of understanding. Standing in what clearly was someone's home, he rested his forehead against what was previously the metal bathroom door in his office. Remembering that this door too, had no lock, yet refused to open.

Sensing a presence in the room, Bill put his hands against the door and slowly turned to face what was waiting for him.

Standing in the center of the living room in front of him was an attractive young woman. Wearing a pair of jeans and sweater, her long, blonde hair draped over one shoulder.

"Hello," Bill opened.

"Hello, Bill," the young woman replied. "And no, you're not hallucinating," reading his thoughts. Continuing on, "Yes, I know your name. You were told to expect me today. Who I am will become clear in a little while."

Realizing once again that it was pointless to keep his thoughts to himself, Bill breathed in deeply and sighed.

"You're in the living room of someone's home. Do you recognize where we are?" the young woman asked.

Looking around, it seemed familiar, but everything was out of context. He was just in his office arguing with his work friend and now he was standing in someone's living room.

"Wait, I'm in one of my rental properties. I recognize it now. I had this new carpet installed five years ago. Odd, it doesn't look any worse for wear."

"That's right," she affirmed. "Do you know who lives here?"

"Yes, it's a woman named Jane, but I don't remember her having any kids."

"She doesn't; the couple living here are the Slatterys. Jane doesn't live here yet," offered the woman.

"Wait," Bill stewed, "the Slatterys lived in this house five years ago. They moved in right after I installed this new carpet..." Just as he was finishing

14

his thought, a young boy tore into the room, flying his toy airplane, heading on a collision course toward the young woman.

"Careful Jacob!" Bill warned, but before he could take a step, the boy ran straight through the young woman, passing through without slowing down.

Eyes widening, "You *ARE* a ghost!" Bill proclaimed loudly.

"Ghost schmost, I guess you could call me that," she chided. "How you refer to me is not as important as what I represent." Young Jacob was still flying around the room defending the Earth from certain destruction, making the appropriate sound effects to chronicle the epic events unfolding.

"Well, the Slatterys only lived in this house for a short period of time, a few months actually. They were really nice people, but now that I think about it, I had to evict them. They just never paid their bills on time." Bill relented, "That was the first eviction I ever had."

"You are correct; the Slatterys lived here with their son who turns 4 years old today," the woman explained.

"Oh, I do remember this. They invited me to his birthday party," Bill remembered. "I couldn't stay long though, I had work to do at the other rental units."

"That's right. And do you remember what happened six weeks later?"

"Yes, I showed up with the sheriff to evict them. It was a horrible day." Bill stared off into the distance, remembering how the events unfolded. "If only they would've paid their rent, I mean, I couldn't let them live here for free. I tried to work with them, but it just got to be too much. At some point, you just have to say enough is enough." Bill felt good justifying this to himself.

"It's not me you have to convince," said the young woman.

Just then, Mrs. Slattery walked into the room and flopped down on the couch, unaware of her invisible house guests. Tears in her eyes, she held a small, white-plastic stick in her hands and stared at it.

"Positive," she whispered to herself. "How on earth am I pregnant?"

Bill looked on, not believing what he was hearing. "Wait, I evicted a pregnant woman?"

"Yep, six weeks from now. At least you got to come here and enjoy some birthday cake," the young woman added. "Come with me."

Walking out of the living room, the woman led Bill to the bathroom just down the hallway. She pointed, directing Bill to go in. "Notice anything?"

Bill looked around; nothing stood out to him. "Not exactly. What is it I'm looking for?"

"Look at the tub faucet," she said.

Looking at the faucet, Bill noticed a thin stream of water coming out. Thinking to himself, "Oh yeah, I think I remember them saying something about that once."

"Four times in three months to be precise," said the young woman. "Go put your hand under the stream of water."

Doing so, Bill noticed immediately the water was leaking from the hot water side. "Well, first of all, I know it wasn't four times, but also, they never told me it was the hot water leaking. I would have made it a higher priority to get it fixed."

"I happen to know it was four times. Would you like me to bring you back to each time she called?" the young woman asked. "I might have to call in a favor from Upstairs, but I can arrange that."

"No, that won't be necessary. I believe you." Bill replied. "I really thought they would have told me if there was a big issue going on with their bills. I certainly would have made a concession if I knew she was expecting."

"But these are your customers; what would have been the difference? It still needed to be fixed." Not waiting for Bill to respond, the young woman produced the previous two months' utility bills for the house.

"Where did you get these?" Bill asked, quickly surveying them. "Oh man, these bills are outrageous!"

"Yes, they are, and it all could have been avoided had you simply done what you said you were going to do. Do you know how much money the Slatterys make each month?" pressed the young woman.

"No, well, not offhand," Bill replied.

"Not very much. In fact, there's no way you would know how much they actually made, because you never had them fill out an application. Yes, you asked for some paystubs, but you never did anything with them. If you had an actual application process and rules in place, it's likely you never would have placed the Slatterys in this house to begin with. They were a young couple just starting out, they had no idea what the cost of things was."

The young woman continued, "You felt that you were doing them a favor by renting to them. All you succeeded in doing was setting them up to fail. Isn't that true, Bill?" The young woman was saying all of this quite plainly, very matter-of-fact.

"Would you like me to show you the folder you put the paystubs in?" she pressed.

"No, you've made your point," Bill conceded.

"In my defense, I *was* busy. It's not like I wasn't doing my best to get over here or sitting around just counting my money on my 'yacht'. I know plenty of landlords who never do anything and just milk their properties. I do the best I can to get to all the repairs as fast as I can. That repair would have cost me hundreds of dollars to have a plumber do it," Bill defended.

"So instead, it cost the Slatterys hundreds of dollars more, twice as much in fact," the young woman noted. "I am quite aware of how busy you were. Since you chose not to make this particular issue a priority, however, it cost you much more. Not only were you not receiving rent because you evicted them, you then had to get the place rent-ready again, right?"

"Well, yeah," Bill agreed.

"Plus, you *still* had to get that leak fixed, didn't you?" the young woman asked.

Nodding, Bill realized he'd done these people wrong. He leveraged his time too much and didn't have any way of tracking when residents were calling in work orders. For that matter, he had no meaningful way to keep track of what needed to be done. He was feeling frustrated and lost, but he wouldn't admit it.

"I know you're feeling frustrated and lost, and you won't admit it," the young woman pointed out. "But, at least you have a good relationship with your tenants, right?"

"Well, yes. That's the one thing I pride myself in," Bill said. "I know all I can about my tenants so I can help take care of them. Plus, I want them to know

I care, so they're more likely to stay with me and keep the rent paid."

"Interesting you say that," the young woman said, nodding. "Come with me to the back yard."

Walking out to the back yard of the home, Bill realized this wasn't the same home they were just in. Mr. Slattery and a very pregnant Mrs. Slattery were sitting on lawn chairs watching their son, Jacob, play in a nearby sandbox.

"So, where are we now?" Correcting himself, "I guess I should ask, *when* are we now?"

"You catch on fast," said the young woman. "It's six months later, and we're in the back yard of Mr. Slattery's parents."

"What are we doing here?" Bill pressed.

"This is where the Slatterys went to live," said the young woman. "Once they were evicted, they had nowhere else to go."

"In this dumpy little place? It's hardly big enough for the three of them," Bill noticed, surveying the size of the house from the outside.

"Well, it's the best they could do," the young woman replied. "With the eviction on their record, no reputable place in town would rent to them. And you're right, it is a dumpy little place, just two bedrooms. Mr. Slattery's parents sleep on the fold out couch in the living room so Mrs. Slattery can have the bedroom. Although she feels terrible about this arrangement, Mrs. Slattery is also incredibly grateful since she is six months into her pregnancy."

"I feel sick to my stomach," Bill confessed. "I wish I didn't know about any of this."

"Ignorance is truly bliss, isn't it?" the young woman asked. "Shush for a second, you need to hear what they're talking about."

Moving closer, it was evident that the Slatterys didn't know about the intruders in their back yard listening in. The Slatterys were holding hands, discussing their future.

"I know it will be tough, but if I take an additional job, we can get the eviction judgement paid so we can get a place of our own," Mr. Slattery explained to his wife. "It will only be for a year or so, and we can get back on our feet. Plus, we still need to pay those outrageous utilities we owe. I'm afraid that is hurting our credit too. Ugh, if only Bill wasn't such a crook."

"Crook?" Bill shouted, "I'm not the one who stole anything!" Continuing on, "If anything, you stole from me!" Bill's comments were unheard by anyone except himself and the young woman.

Mrs. Slattery responded to her husband, "Honey, Bill was a liar, we had no reason to think that he would pull the rug out from under us the way he did. He always promised to come fix stuff and never did."

"I thought we were friends," Mr. Slattery explained. "It really hurt the way he turned his back on us. I mean, we had him over for dinner; heck, we even had him at Jacob's birthday party. He took the time to get to know us and act like our friend. What kind of friend *does* that?"

Mrs. Slattery chimed in, "We both thought the same thing, honey. We thought we could trust him to do what he said he would. I could deal with all the little stuff we needed fixed, but it was the leak in the bathtub that hurt the most. The inflated water bill, plus all the electricity it took to heat all that wasted hot water. That really put us under financially. He acted like such a great guy – until he wanted his money."

Bill stood listening, not believing what impression he had given the Slatterys. "Is that what they really think? That I was their friend? That I lied to them?"

The young woman answered, "It sure seems that way, doesn't it? That is *their* reality. You made their experience so personal that they were confused."

"I just thought I was being a good landlord, offering good, friendly customer service," said Bill.

"So, you think good customer service is about being friendly to the point of being overly familiar?" asked the young woman.

Bill answered her immediately, "No, It's about doing what you say you will do."

"What if it really is that simple?" she asked rhetorically.

Bill sat quietly, considering all he had seen and heard. It was hard to swallow. He'd been a landlord for a while now. He felt he knew all there was to know. He knew he had shortcomings, but who didn't?

After a while, Bill realized he didn't know how to refer to the young woman, now sitting on the picnic table watching Jacob play. "You never did tell me your name," Bill pointed out.

"Well," she paused, "earlier you referred to me as a ghost right?"

"Yes," Bill nodded.

"I represent all your past tenants," she declared.

"So, you're the Ghost of Tenants-Past?" Bill sputtered slowly.

Laughing, "Sure!" the young woman said of her new moniker. "That'll work. However, I'm afraid our time together is done. I need to make sure you're back in time."

"Wait," Bill pleaded. "I don't know that I'm ready to go back. I mean, what became of the Slatterys?"

"You'll find out when it's time," said the young woman. "But now we've got to go. I promised to have you back. Can't break our promises with the Big Guy."

"Wait, what do I have to be back for?" Bill asked.

"Again, you'll find out soon enough," she assured him. "We do need to go, though. Jacob is about to do something a little gross, and I don't think you're going to want to be here for this."

"What do you mean?" Bill asked. Just then, he noticed Jacob taking his little sand shovel and switching from picking up and flinging sand, to a large pile of wet dog droppings.

"Oh no, Jacob, no!" Bill whispered out loud. Jacob, as if he could see Bill, started toward Bill with the poop-laden shovel, laughing and giggling as he picked up speed.

"Did I mention that sometimes kids can see us?" the young woman lamented.

"Mr. Bill! Mr. Bill!" shouted Jacob. Mrs. Slattery, oblivious to what Jacob was doing, said "That's right, honey, Daddy and I are talking about Mr. Bill."

As Jacob runs toward Bill with the shovel-full of wet poo, Bill and the young woman scatter in opposite directions of the yard.

Bill, cornered in the fenced yard, looking at Jacob charging at him, shouts, "No Jacob, no!"

"Mr. Bill!" Jacob cheers, rearing the shovel back, ready to fling its sloppy payload.

"NO! Jacob, NO!" commands Bill, wincing, preparing for the worst.

In one last, desperate request, Bill cries out, "No! Do NOT throw poop on me!"

Just as the last sentence left his mouth, Bill, still wincing and half-crouched, got the sense that he was no longer in the Slattery's back yard. Carefully opening his eyes, one at a time, he was back at work, standing in the bathroom again. A few of his coworkers were standing in front of him with puzzled looks on their faces.

Bill stood up straight and looked around at all of them. No one knew what to say. Finally, one of them broke the awkward silence.

"Well, we're all under a lot of stress, Bill." The man said, pausing, thinking of his next words. "And while I'm pretty sure it's not specifically spelled out in the employee handbook, I think it's understood that we're not to throw poop at anyone in the office."

It was Tony from Human Resources, of all people. "Right everyone? We all agree we're not going to throw poop on Bill."

The few men in the restroom nodded, agreeing with the H.R. director. Moving toward the door, the men started filing out. Bill heard one of the men whisper as they left the restroom, "Does he think we work at the zoo?"

Chapter Two

Bill was back in his office, sitting at his desk, trying to figure out what all of this was about. It was a few minutes after 9 a.m., but it felt like he'd been at work for hours. He didn't know what was happening to him, or why, for that matter, but if what became of the Slatterys was true, then he needed to do something about it.

A puff of smoke filtered through the air over Bill's head, indicating once again, he had a visitor.

The thick accent of The Judge broke the silence of Bill's solitude. "So Governor," which he pronounced 'Guv-Na', "What'd you think of old sassy britches?"

"Beautiful lady, or uh, ghost, I guess," Bill fumbled. He still wasn't sure how to refer to his guests.

"Doesn't matter a bit of difference to me, son," The Judge explained, "it's whatever you need us to be."

"Okay, I guess it doesn't matter. But seriously, what is going on? I am being flashed around in some sort of weird time-space continuum. You appear and disappear as you please, my coworkers think I'm losing my damn mind, and I'm probably going to lose my job before the end of the day. Can you please tell me what all of this is about?"

The Judge took a long draw on his fat cigar. "This is a Gran Corona, I never knew much about cigars except that I like them. Now that I have access to the good ones, I enjoy them even more," he grinned, taking the cigar from his mouth and admiring it.

The Judge continued, "The reason I'm here, son, is because honestly, and let me be clear, you're about to mix sugar in your grits and pour brown gravy all over your sweet corn. I'm trying to get you some learning done before the mongoose gets in the snake-house. You follow?"

Bill blinked, "I have no idea what you just said…"

Squinting his eyes through the thick smoke of his cigar firmly lodged in his mouth, The Judge concluded, "Son… you're a hot damned mess."

"Forget about the 'why' here for a second," said The Judge. "What did you learn from your visit today with sassy britches?"

"Well, I learned I really messed up with the Slatterys. They're good people, but I guess they are feeling that I pretty well screwed them over."

"That's right, and do you blame them?" The Judge pressed.

"Honestly, no. I guess I just never thought about how they would be affected by my, well…" Bill paused.

"Go ahead, I already know what you're thinking but *YOU* need to say it," said The Judge.

"…my lack of organization," Bill reluctantly confessed.

"Hot Damn, I think we might actually be getting somewhere with you, young man," The Judge clasped his hands. "That's right, but maybe a better word than organization would be infrastructure. Son, let's face it; you have none," The Judge pointed out.

"Well, true, I guess I don't have much infrastructure to speak of, but it's not like I'm a big operation either," Bill pointed out.

"Who says you need to be a big operation to have infrastructure?" The Judge continued, motioning to Bill to settle in for the first lesson:

"Fire Yourself First."

The Judge pressed his point, "When it comes to working your business, you need to constantly be thinking of ways to remove yourself as the person who 'does all the doing'. You have to build infrastructure to free yourself, task by task."

"Well, I guess that's true. But it's not like I have a ton of money to invest in infrastructure. With the tenants not paying rent very consistently and the constant repairs I need to do, there's not much left over for paying mortgages, let alone paying for infrastructure," Bill explained. "I *have* to do all the work."

"Ah, I see. Well, let's go over the Slatterys biggest complaints." The Judge instructed.

"Well first they said I lied to them."

"You think *that* was their biggest complaint? Why are you making this about *you*?" The Judge asked. "Stop making this about you; it's about *them*."

"Okay, you're right. So, if they're feeling as if I lied to them, it's because I didn't do what I said I'd do. Specifically, things weren't addressed fast enough."

"Very good, Bill, I agree with that whole statement. Primarily, you didn't do what you said you'd do.

Now, let's reach a bit deeper under the hen and pull out the egg; what could you have done differently to address these problems?"

"I don't know. Honestly, half the time when they called I spent more time talking to them about other stuff and I'd forget to write down their maintenance problems," Bill sat thoughtfully. "I've had an idea for a while now, but I never really thought it was necessary."

"Go ahead, let's talk it through," The Judge prodded Bill.

"Well, I've considered hiring a Virtual Assistant, or VA, to help me with stuff. I even looked into the cost, and they're actually pretty reasonable." Bill contemplated for a minute. "I could set up a different number for my tenants to contact my VA for everything."

"Everything like what?" The Judge prompted. "Be more specific."

"Well, everything from maintenance requests to prospects wanting to see a vacant unit. I could give the VA my personal number in case of emergencies. But otherwise, they could take messages for me and organize any outstanding work orders that are called in." Bill seemed to be on a roll.

"Okay, I like where this is going. What else?" The Judge pressed.

"Well, I suppose if I had a vacant unit, the VA could set appointments for me too, and answer some basic questions about the property based on a written description I could send them."

"Now you're thinking. By firing yourself from those low-dollar tasks, you're making better use of your time," The Judge encouraged Bill.

Bill went on, "I could even get the VA to research vendors for me and contact them directly if the tenant calls in a problem I know I can't handle, like plumbing or electrical stuff. I could put a list together of stuff the VA is pre-approved to call a vendor for on my behalf."

The Judge was impressed. "Excellent, do you realize what else this will help you with?"

Bill sat for a moment, "Well, not really; what am I missing?"

"Think about it. What was one of the other criticisms that the Slatterys had about you?"

"Well, they said I was a liar, but that was because I didn't fix stuff in a timely manner. Honestly though, I either didn't write it down, or I just plain forgot," Bill openly admitted. "As I think about it, I would leave the house Saturday morning trying to think about who called during the week. It was not a good system."

"Well, now it looks like we're getting some traction," The Judge said happily. "But what was the real basis of the criticism that they had for you; you're dancing around and not saying it."

"Well, something the Slatterys said really bothered me, specifically Mrs. Slattery. She said 'I was a great guy until I wanted my money.' I have to be honest, that was like a punch in the gut," Bill admitted to The Judge.

"Why do you think that was so hurtful?"

"I don't know, maybe because I felt so close to them. When Mr. Slattery said 'I thought we were friends' it made me think that maybe I got a little *too* close to them. When he said how he felt when I turned my back on them, I realized for the first time maybe that was the case."

The Judge blew smoke into the air incredulously, "Maybe? *Maybe*, you were too close? You were invited to their kid's birthday party and had dinner at their house for crying out loud!"

"Okay, so I got too close to them. But it's not like that with all my tenants. I really think I have a solid relationship with all my other tenants, especially my current ones. I think I've set a pretty clear boundary," Bill spoke confidently.

The Judge stewed for a minute. "Funny you should say that, about your current tenants, that is. It's about time for your next meeting. We're on a tight timeline today."

"Tight timeline?" Bill looked down at his watch. "It's still just after 9:00 a.m."

"I know, but the Big Guy runs a tight ship. Let's get you to your next meeting." The Judge took a long draw from his cigar. Walking up to Bill, he blew the smoke from his long draw directly in his face. Bill closed his eyes out of reflex. "See you again real soon, son."

Chapter Three

Blinking his eyes open, Bill was sitting at a kitchen table in someone's home. Having been through this once before, he figured he was sitting in one of his rental properties.

"You would be correct in that assumption," the voice came from across the table.

"Hello," Bill greeted the man. "Where exactly are we?" Bill paused, "or should I ask 'when' are we?" He offered a lopsided grin to his guest.

The man sitting across the table from Bill was middle-aged, bald on top, and significantly overweight. He had a plate of pancakes sitting in front of him that he looked like he was ready to devour.

"I was told you're a quick study; you're asking the right questions, at least," the bald man answered. "Look around. This should all be very familiar to you," he said, pointing around with his fork.

Bill looked around, agreeing with the bald man. "It does; it looks very familiar. In fact, I was here only yesterday fixing some stuff. It's a unit with a grandma, a single mom, and her adult son and teenage daughter. I know the Stewarts quite well, they are good people. We're very close; I'd almost consider them friends."

The bald man, using the side of his fork, started cutting into his pancakes, slicing through the healthy pile of strawberries and roughly three inches of whipped cream which had appeared. A grin appeared on the man's face, indicating the pure, anticipated-joy he was about to experience.

"This is what I love about these assignments," the bald man mused, sighing heavily as he chomped his food with an open mouth.

"What's that?" Bill asked, "Breakfast?"

"Not just breakfast – pancakes!" the bald man said with a full mouth. "Pancakes represent all that is right with the world."

"So, what are we doing in the Stewart's kitchen?" Bill said curiously.

Finishing his first bite, the bald man paused, "Well, why do you think?"

"I honestly don't know. I mean, I seem to understand all of this visiting has to do with the way I'm running my rental business. But with the Stewarts, well, they always seem pretty happy to me." Bill knitted his brow, considering the bald man's question intently.

"Well, you're partly right," said the bald man, resting his fork. "This does have to do with the way your business is being run. Come with me."

Picking up his plate and walking into the next room, Ms. Stewart was sitting at the dining room table in front of a pile of newspapers and mail. Plopping down at the other end of the table, the bald man resumed devouring his meal.

"What's she doing?" Bill asked, scanning the mess of papers around him.

"Trying to make ends meet," the bald man said with his cheeks full of food.

"How could that possibly be? Grandma collects social security, Ms. Stewart is a nurse, and it's just her adult son and daughter," Bill stated. "I mean, it sounds like they should be doing very well."

"And how would you know that?" the bald man asked sincerely.

Bill thought for a second, realizing his ignorance. "I don't," he confessed.

"That's right! And, why don't you know?" the bald man fired back, pointing his fork at Bill, stabbing it in the air to emphasize his words.

"Because I never had her complete an application. I honestly don't know much about her besides her paystubs and her mom's Social Security letter," Bill admitted.

Finishing his last bite of pancakes, and wiping his mouth with the tablecloth, the bald man asserted, "Doesn't seem to be a great way to run a rental business."

"Well, I confirmed their income," Bill defended. "They make a lot more than the rent each month. Someone told me once that three times the rent amount in income is a good rule of thumb."

"Okay, that is a good rule of thumb, I suppose. But the income is just one side of the equation, isn't it?" The bald man said, cleaning his hands on his shirt.

"Well, yeah, and expenses is the other side," Bill answered.

"And what do you know about her expenses?" the bald man prodded.

"Absolutely nothing; I see that now," Bill relented. "Without that sort of information, I could be setting these people up to fail. Someone just pointed that out to me."

"Great way to put it. Having a well-thought-out application process would make a lot more sense and not set anyone up to fail," the bald man agreed. "At a minimum, a basic understanding of their monthly obligations would be a good start."

Bill went on, "I just need to find a way to check their credit and get public record information so I know what I'm dealing with and what their past looks like."

"Super easy in the information age. Charging the applicant an application fee covers the cost of the getting the information. Plus, it ensures you get only the people who are serious."

Bill chewed on that idea. "I've never charged an application fee. I never saw any need to."

The bald man agreed, "There *wasn't* any need to; you didn't *have* an application!"

"Well... true," Bill said, feeling bad; disappointed in his mistakes.

"Look, don't feel bad or disappointed in your mistakes. You've made a lot of mistakes, but it seems like you're sincere in changing your ways." He put a hand up to Bill to pause his thoughts, "Hang on, you're going to want to hear what's about to happen."

"Mom!" the daughter hollered from the back of the house, "The bathroom light won't come on again!"

Ms. Stewart hollered back without looking up, "Jiggle the switch!"

"I did jiggle it!" the daughter exclaimed.

Grandma chimed in, "Jiggle the handle!"

"Ma, it's the light, not the toilet this time," Ms. Stewart explained to her mother.

"Mom! It's still not working!" The daughter shouted.

Grandma chimed back in "Is the toilet fixed now?"

"Is the bulb out?" Ms. Stewart hollered back to her daughter.

"Maybe it's the circuit breaker-fuse thing again," Grandma offered. "Now that I think about it, why is the dryer making that awful squealing sound? I did a load of laundry, and I thought your cat got up inside there."

"Grandma, we don't have a cat," the son explained politely.

"Don't we? What happened to your cat?" Grandma asked her daughter.

"Ma! We never had a cat!" Ms. Stewart yelled.

The frenetic scene continued on for a few more minutes, the lava inside Ms. Stewart simmering to a slow boil, as she tried to stay focused on her budget for the next week.

"Why don't you get that nice man back out here to fix a few things?" Grandma asked sweetly.

"He was just here Ma; we probably won't see him here again for a while," Ms. Stewart explained to her mother.

"Well, just tell him we have some more things to fix. He's such a nice man, I'm sure he'll come right out," Grandma continued. "Plus, I think he's single!"

"You had to throw that in there, didn't you?" Ms. Stewart chirped back.

Grandma was giggling; she couldn't help herself. "I'm just saying, it would be nice to have a man around here to fix some things."

"Mom, seriously," her daughter pleaded, "I'm going to be late for Justin to pick me up. Can you please come get this light working!"

At her wit's end, smacking her hands on the table, Ms. Stewart pushed herself to her feet and marched down the hallway. Getting to the bathroom, she knew how to pull the light switch just the right way – up and to the left – to get the bathroom light to come to life.

She walked back down the hallway to return to her bills. Grandma started back in at the sight of her daughter, "Do you want me to get Bill on the phone for you? He's so nice, and I see how nice you are back to him."

Exhausted, Ms. Stewart barked back, "Ma, I'm nice to him because it's easier to get him out here that way. I really can't stand the guy."

"Yeah, Bill is lame." Her daughter chimed in, applying makeup in the bathroom down the hall.

"He never does anything he says he's going to do. It's just easier to be nice to him so things get done."

"That's not nice to talk about adults that way sweetheart!" Ms. Stewart hollered, condemning her daughter's statement. *"Even if it is true,"* she said under her breath.

Bill stood taking it all in, incredulous at what he just witnessed. The bald man, realizing Bill could use a break, stood behind him. "Come on, let me buy you some pancakes." Bill nodded, and within a blink, he was sitting across from the bald man at an unfamiliar table.

Looking around, he saw a lot of tables but no one else there. Bill had no idea where he was.

"It's the best place you'll ever eat at. Impossible to get reservations, but the food is amazing – some would say heavenly," the bald man explained. "I thought it would be good to retreat to a neutral place for a bit."

"Thanks, it's been a crazy day," Bill admitted, noticing a stack of pancakes had appeared in front of the bald man. Wasting no time, he dug right in.

"Ahhh…" the bald man sighed, "Pure ambrosia. Now *this* is what I'm talking about."

"What makes these pancakes so special?" Bill asked.

"Not pancakes, Man-cakes," his hungry host corrected. "They may look like regular pancakes, but no sir, these… are Man-cakes."

Playing along, Bill asked, "Okay, I'll go for the bait, what are Man-cakes?"

"Mixed in with the batter," the bald man said excitedly, "are chunks of cooked, spicy breakfast sausage. The sausage is cooked first, then cut and crumbled up into pieces. The sausage pieces are then mixed into the pancake batter. Serve them with some butter and a little syrup. Oh man, it's a license to print money right there."

"You get awfully excited about pancakes." Bill smiled, "You get more excited about pancakes than I do about anything."

"I think that's part of your problem Bill," the bald man said, stopping to savor his meal for a moment. After swallowing his mouthful, he put his fork down and leaned forward on the table. "Now I know this isn't part of my job, and our time together is coming to an end here shortly, but let me ask you something. I need you to really think about this before you answer."

"Okay, shoot." Bill was eager to hear what the bald man had to say.

The bald man thought for a moment, framing his question carefully. "It seems you don't get excited by much because you don't have the time to get excited by much. All you've done with your rental business is create another job for yourself."

Bill nodded in reply. He used all of his time away from work, his free-time, to work in his rental business.

"So, here's my question," the bald man continued, "if you don't put a value on your free-time, who will?"

Bill thought for a minute, "Well, the obvious answer, I guess, would be no one."

"That's right! If you don't put a value on your free-time, nobody else will. Or at least, if someone else did put a value on it for you, it's going to be very low, probably lower than what you would value it, wouldn't you agree?" the bald man smiled, making his point.

"Oh, I definitely agree. They're valuing my free-time less, because they value their free-time more," Bill stated flatly.

"Well," the bald man resumed eating, "I don't know if I agree entirely. I think it has more to do with establishing boundaries and having a system in place, infrastructure, if you will – having something in place to help to systematically handle your customer's most common needs. You follow what I'm saying?"

"Yeah, I know exactly what you're saying. Infrastructure is a word I've been thinking a lot about today," said Bill. "But let me ask, what do you mean by establishing boundaries?"

"Great question, but I think it's a better question answered by someone else. It's about time I got you back."

"Well, thanks for the trip, oh, and the Man-cake recipe. So, can I assume you're the Ghost of Tenants-Present?" Bill was amused.

"Um, sure," the bald man laughed. "Okay, let's get you back."

In an instant, Bill was back, sitting in his office. Leaning forward in his chair, he put his head in his hands, trying his best to process it all. The distinctly southern accent broke the silence.

"You've had quite of learning day so far haven't you, young man?" The Judge asked.

"I'll admit, it's been a lot to process," Bill sighed, "sobering to say the least."

"So, you had a question about boundaries, from what I understand." The Judge said.

"Well, yeah. During my most recent visit, we got talking about free-time. It was in that context we started talking about establishing boundaries."

"And you're trying to figure out what having boundaries means in regard to your customers, right?" The Judge asked. "Well, Bill, what do you think establishing boundaries means?"

"You mean with my tenants? I don't know; I guess it would mean letting them know what is and what isn't acceptable," Bill guessed.

The Judge nodded, "I agree. And to go one step further, boundaries should *never* be violated." He put simply,

"Boundaries Set You Free."

The Judge using his cigar to point toward Bill to drive the point home.

The Judge continued, "Let me ask you something, think of your favorite business where you spend a considerable amount of time. Maybe a restaurant, a barber, maybe even your bank..."

Bill looked intently, "Okay... I'd have to say there's a coffee shop I go to a lot."

"Okay great, now think about why you go there. What's so special to you about this particular place?"

"They have good food, a friendly wait staff, they have WIFI so I can do work if I want to. Plus, they don't mind if I sit there for several hours at a time, and it's on my way home from work. There are a lot of reasons I go there," Bill listed using one finger at time.

"Excellent, and what are their hours?" The Judge nodded, puffing his cigar.

"They open at 7:00 a.m. and close at 7 p.m.," Bill stated.

"So, they're only open 12 hours? That doesn't seem so great."

"Well yeah, but that doesn't really change anything for me. And I don't think it's an issue for any of their other customers either," Bill defended his turf.

"So, what you're saying is, even though it's only open 12 hours, it doesn't affect your customer service experience?" The Judge asked.

"No, not at all," said Bill. "I guess in some ways, it makes the experience better because they're more focused on being good at what they want to be good at. They do great breakfast and lunch, but they don't do dinner."

"But if I had to guess, and you know I don't, you let your tenants call and text you at all hours of the day and night, don't you?" The Judge asked rhetorically.

Bill nodded in reply.

The Judge stood up. "Young man, I need you to pay close attention to something I'm about to say: Boundaries set us free. The owners of that restaurant set boundaries, a lot of boundaries, whether you realize it or not." The Judge pointed out. "They establish open and closing times, whether you can pay by cash, check, or credit card, even if you can substitute french fries for cole slaw, right?"

"Well yeah, I guess I never really thought about it that way," Bill said.

"Do you have the owner's cell phone number?" The Judge asked.

"Well, no," Bill replied.

"And why is that? Why don't they give out their cell phone number to every customer?"

"Boundaries," Bill said plainly, understanding the lesson.

"That's right, son," the Judge smirked, happy with his pupil. "That's the way you need to approach your business relationship with your tenants. Now that the horse is out of the barn, the toughest thing for you will be getting them used to you not picking up the phone every time they feel like calling. They won't like boundaries at first, but they'll get used to it."

The Judge continued, "But, you have to be consistent; you can't answer the phone on a Sunday one week and not do it another, for example. That's only going to create confusion and disrupt the whole system."

Bill interrupted, "A problem that could be eliminated entirely by having someone else answer the phone, during set business hours, for example."

"Exactly, so consider getting another cell phone for your friends and family and disconnect your current number. Get another number set up for your tenants and forward it to a virtual assistant who will answer calls from your current and prospective customers. All of this will likely cost a few hundred dollars at the most," The Judge advised. "Pretty cheap, yet effective, infrastructure if you ask me."

"And, if I can add to that, I can give my VA specific instructions and guidelines to follow, and times when I am to be contacted, emergencies, for example," Bill said intently. He was starting to show he understood.

"That's right Bill. This is all very good. But there's one more thing you're not considering about how this infrastructure will help. It's a problem we haven't talked about yet," The Judge warned. "It's actually the most significant problem you face, and you haven't said it yet."

"If you're talking about my relationship with my tenants, yeah I get it. I get too close to them emotionally," Bill admitted.

"Here, let me give you an analogy." The Judge sat in the chair across from Bill, who was still sitting at his desk. "You're pretty close with your brother, right?"

"Yes, an older brother. He and I have a good relationship," Bill reported.

"Okay, good. Let's say you borrowed $500 from your brother, and at the same time you borrowed $500 from the bank. Now to keep things simple here we're just going to say that both loans are due at the same time, one month from now. So, all things being equal, if you only had enough money to pay one loan when it came due, who are you most likely to pay?"

"Well, my brother can be a jerk, but I'd probably pay the bank. I could always talk to my brother and try to make other arrangements or ask him to work with me. The bank, well, they just don't care," Bill noted.

"That's right, and what would happen if you didn't pay the bank?" The Judge asked.

"Well, they'd start calling me at home and at work. They'd send me notices of default. I suppose, eventually, they'd take me to court and garnish my wages. Not to mention they would wreck my credit," Bill said, trying to think of all the possibilities.

"And why is that; why would the bank do all this?"

"Because they don't care!" Bill laughed, "Sad to say, but it's true."

The Judge argued, "It's not so much that they don't care, but the bank has something that your brother doesn't. We've been talking about it all morning."

"Let me guess, infrastructure?" Bill guessed correctly.

"That's right," The Judge agreed. "I'm sure you have a good relationship with your banker, but 'the bank' doesn't make the distinction. There is no emotional attachment. If you don't pay your brother, he might even forget to call you about it until he's short on money. In the bank's case, they'll likely call you on the first day the loan is delinquent!"

"So, is that the other reason to develop infrastructure, so I can provide an emotional buffer between myself and my tenants?" Bill asked.

"It's surely a good reason," The Judge answered. "It's certainly why property managers have a job. They help keep real estate investors focused on the business of investing, not getting bogged down in the operations which can suck a lot of emotional energy."

"I don't know if I really need that though. I mean, I think I have a pretty thick skin for this stuff," Bill thought out loud.

The Judge laughed, "No offense son, but I've seen thicker skin on chocolate pudding."

"Look, not everyone is cut out for landlording, I saw that all the time from the bench," The Judge remembered.

The Judge continued his thought, "I always regarded how difficult it must be for private landlords to operate when they are the salesperson, accountant, collections department, and maintenance technician."

Bill snorted, "You just described me!"

"Well, I say it's difficult for these private landlords to change hats from one capacity to the next. But I'd say the biggest difficulty isn't so much on the landlord, it's for the tenant. The tenant never knows 'which guy' is calling."

The Judge pressed on, "So as a result, everything gets to be quite a jumble. It may not be a problem for the landlord to separate business from private life, but for the tenant, it's easy to get confused."

Bill thought back to Mrs. Slattery's statement, "Bill acts like such a great guy, until he wants his money."

"Yeah, what a crazy thing to say, as if you needing money to pay your bills was some sort of obscenity," The Judge defended Bill.

"Yeah, so is this the significant problem you're talking about? That my tenants don't pay me on time because I'm too familiar with them?" Bill asked.

"I think it's about time you get to your next appointment. You're going to need to see it for yourself. I'll be here when you get back." The Judge assured him.

Bill readied himself, leaned back in his chair, and closed his eyes. He knew he'd be opening them to different surroundings yet again.

Chapter Four

True to the theme of the day, Bill opened his eyes to a similar, but different, workplace. Looking around, he found himself seated at a desk surrounded by a sea of cubicles. His office was gone, now replaced by more spartan surroundings. It appeared that Bill, no longer a manager, had joined the cubicle dwellers.

A young girl appeared before him, maybe 10 years old, with long reddish hair and pale skin. She wore a pretty red dress made of velvet.

"Okay, so I assume I'm in the future, right?"

The girl smiled gently, and nodded once.

"Great," he thought. "So, you're the Ghost of Tenants-Future. Where are we anyway?"

The office, bustling with people on the phone, was some sort of call center. Looking around, he saw his personal items had been organized neatly in the cubicle where he sat. "Wait, are we at what becomes a new job for me? How is this possible?"

The girl pointed to his jacket pocket. Following her direction, Bill reached inside and pulled out his cell phone. She tilted her head and smiled plainly at him.

"All my tenants calling my cell phone during the work day got me fired," Bill thought.

The girl blinked as she nodded.

"Wow, unbelievable. I really can't believe I lost my job over that," Bill said to himself. "Jessica was right. She even tried to warn me," he sat, thinking of his work friend and their conversation earlier that morning.

The girl smiled, turned, and started walking down the sea of cubicles. Bill, not knowing what to do and not wanting to be left there, followed the girl as she navigated the labyrinth.

Bill zig-zagged his way through the maze of cubicles. The girl moved quickly, staying well ahead of him. Bill turned the last corner and found himself standing in the front yard of one of his rental homes.

Taking in the scene, he noticed right away how good the house looked. He bought it originally as a fixer-upper, but never had the time to do all the repairs he wanted to before he started renting it.

"Wow, so this is what becomes of this house? That's cool; I always wanted to get this house fixed up and looking better. I'm glad to see it in such good shape," Bill smiled.

The girl pointed to the 'For Rent' sign in the yard.

Turning, Bill read the sign out loud "ABC Rentals, LLC?" Bill couldn't believe his eyes. "Those guys are renting my house!"

The girl nodded to Bill.

"I don't understand; how did they get my house? I never wanted to sell this place." Bill was confused. "I certainly never would have sold it to those guys!"

Bill barely got the question out when he again had a change of scenery. This time, he was in a small apartment. It was not one he recognized, certainly not one he'd been in before. Looking around, he noticed some familiar things. After a few minutes, he realized everything in this small apartment belonged to him. Furniture, pictures, pots and pans – all of it. Somehow all of his stuff, at least all that would fit, had been moved from his spacious, three-bedroom house into this cramped, one-bedroom apartment.

"Wait, is this where I live now?" Bill cried. "What happened to me? What caused all this?"

The girl stood in the tiny kitchen, pointing to the only table in the small apartment. There, sat a stack of mail, still unopened. All of it was addressed to him.

Bill walked slowly over to the table, picking up one piece of mail. Nearly all were thick and heavy, with return addresses from law firms. Tearing open the first envelope, he realized what it was.

"These are all medical bills," he paused for a second, "I must've gotten sick at some point." He stopped to think about his level of involvement with his rental properties. It all fell on him to do everything. He picked up another piece of mail.

"This one is a Notice of Foreclosure," Bill exclaimed. "Holy moly, look at all this mail! And all of these are legal notices. That explains why I live here in this place in the future. Am I really going to lose everything?"

The girl looked at him emotionless, shrugging her shoulders slowly.

"I can't believe this," Bill whispered. He leaned back onto the refrigerator, sliding down until he was sitting on the floor, the legal notice still in his hand. "Everything I worked for is gone."

He sat solemnly, trying to digest everything he learned throughout the day. All the talk of infrastructure and boundaries and overfamiliarity. He was embarrassed by it, thinking it was all so simple, yet he was about to lose it all.

He thought of The Judge; what was the purpose behind all of this if he was going to lose his properties, and his job, regardless of what he did?

"Wait a second," Bill thought. "The Judge said he came here before it was too late," Bill's attention turned to the girl.

"You didn't nod your head yes!" He exclaimed.

The girl, not understanding, squinted her eyes at him, tilting her head to one side seeking an explanation.

"I asked you a minute ago if I'm really going to lose everything and you shrugged your shoulders," Bill said slowly. "You didn't nod your head 'yes'," thinking out loud.

"So, I can still save myself from losing all my properties, isn't that right?"

The girl smiled while she nodded slowly.

Excited, Bill jumped up. "Well, hot damn! C'mon, I have to get back. I've got a lot of work to do!"

The girl smiled broadly, and in an instant, Bill was sent back.

Standing back in his office, Bill was charged up and ready to get things in place. "Judge?" he called out, turning around, "Judge, where are you?"

The Judge appeared behind him, sitting at Bill's desk with his feet propped up on it, leaning back, and blowing smoke rings into the air. "You seem encouraged," said The Judge in his thick southern drawl. "I wasn't sure what to expect from you after this last visit."

"Funny, I thought you knew everything," Bill chided.

"I might be able to read your thoughts, but I can't know if you're going to change your mind. That's entirely up to you. Only experience and learning will do that." The Judge confided.

"I'll admit, I never put much stock in education after college. I guess I just felt I knew all I needed to know about my job." Bill sulked. "I figured my real estate business was just doing things that seemed to be common sense. Before today, I have to admit, I didn't know what I didn't know."

"But now, at least you *know* what you don't know, right?" The Judge encouraged Bill. "Or, at least some of it."

"Definitely, I mean, there's probably so much more I need to learn. I see that now," Bill said humbly.

"I think now you're getting it son," The Judge paused, "so, why don't you tell me the last lesson?"

Bill paused for a second; there was so much running through his head. But this entire experience taught him something that he had long forgotten:

"Lean Into Learning."

"I like it," said The Judge. "Not sure I could've said it any better."

"So where do I go from here? I mean, I've got some ideas, but I can't say a few moments of clarity has suddenly made me an expert. And clearly, something needs to be done right away. I've got a lot of disappointed people out there I need to reach out to."

"Son, I can't tell you what to do specifically, because it's your business.   Become a student again; read all you can about businesses that run well, even if those businesses have nothing to do with rentals."

"Look, I'm due back but I want to leave you with a final thought."   The judge continued, "You're a good man, that is clear. You'll figure it out. Read all you can. Find yourself a mentor. No matter what, the best thing you can do when it comes to learning is to have an open mind," The Judge said, his eyes expressing his sincerity.

For a moment, the two locked eyes and smiled, student to teacher, bidding each other farewell as their studies together concluded.

"Take care, Son," The Judge winked. And with that, he was gone.

Looking around his office, Bill sighed heavily at all he'd learned today. For the first time in a while, Bill was finally alone. Reflecting on his day, he realized he had a lot to do – and even more to learn. He knew he had some 'fences to mend', as The Judge might say. Bill smiled at his own cleverness as he walked out of his office.

The office had returned to its normal hustle and bustle. Walking fast and with purpose, he searched for his office friend, marching into her office without knocking.

"Jessica!" Bill announced excitedly.

"Hey Bill, sheesh you startled me. Are you okay? H.R. just called me asking if I knew if you were doing alright." Pausing for a second, "My gosh, you're pale. You look like you've seen a ghost!"

"Well, several actually," Bill explained quickly. "Although one is still up for debate," he mused to himself. "Look, Jessica, I wanted to thank you for watching out for me, and for trying to help me. I was wrong."

Perplexed by his answer, Jessica realized he was apologizing. Bill always marched to his own drummer, but this was different. She was concerned for her work friend, although something told her he would be okay. Before she realized it, Bill was excusing himself from her office and heading back down the hallway.

Stopping by H.R., Bill felt he owed Tony an apology for his unusual behavior earlier. They had a good laugh and promised to have lunch soon. Then, he headed back to his office. Picking up his cell phone, he dialed in and quickly changed his voicemail message. His new message explained that he would be monitoring his voicemails, but unless it was an emergency, he would be returning calls after 5:00 p.m. He planned to put something more permanent in place, but he needed to get focused on his work. This was the quickest thing he could do right away. Bill looked at his phone and smiled, "Boundaries."

He looked at the clock; 9:15 a.m. He had a lot of work to get done at the office, and a lot more to do for his tenants. Sitting for a moment, reflecting, he looked on the white board in his office where something had been written.

It was a message.

Fire Yourself First

Boundaries Set You Free

Lean Into Learning

- The Judge

Bill grinned, reflecting on his lessons for the day, gathering his thoughts. His cell phone sat face up, staring at him. He'd already had a long day, but he had one more thing to do.

Bill picked up the phone and dialed. A once-familiar voice answered the phone. Bill cleared his throat,

"Hello, Mrs. Slattery?"

A Final Thought.

When I think of where I'm at in life, I'm reminded of the story of a box turtle on a fence post. You know he didn't get there by himself.

No man is an island. The best performers always have someone they can bounce ideas off of and coach them when they need it. This applies to professional athletes, executives, managers, and entrepreneurs alike.

I would argue that no one *needs* a coach. They will, however, get you to your destination much faster. If you are using one, great. If you aren't and would like to, let's chat. Please go to LandlordCoach.com and send me a message. I'd love to hear from you.

Resources:

The Time-Wealthy Investor: Your Real Estate Roadmap to Owning More, Working Less, and Creating the Life You Want – Available on Amazon, in paperback or audiobook

Also, check out LandlordCoach.com_for other resources, such as the blog page, seminars in your area, as well as instructional videos on how to set up a scalable business that doesn't run your life.

Finally, follow us on the Landlord Coach Facebook page for inspirational messages and keeping up with best practices.

I look forward to seeing your success. Keep your foot on the gas!